The Let's Talk Library™

Let's Talk About Adoption

Diana Star Helmer

The Rosen Publishing Group's
PowerKids Press™
New York

Published in 1999 by The Rosen Publishing Group, Inc.
29 East 21st Street, New York, NY 10010

Copyright © 1999 by The Rosen Publishing Group, Inc.

First Edition

Book Design: Erin McKenna

Photo Credits: p. 7 © Vladimir Pcholikin/FPG International, p. 12 © Ron Chappel/FPG International, p. 15 © Dick Luria/FPG International, p. 16 © Michael Krasowitz/FPG International, p. 19 © Arthur Tilley/FPG International.

Photo Illustrations: Cover and pp. 4, 8, 11, 20 by Seth Dinnerman.

Helmer, Diana Star.
    Let's talk about adoption / by Diana Star Helmer.
        p.   cm.— (The let's talk library)
    Includes index.
    Summary: Explains what adoption is, why a parent might put a child up for adoption, and what is special about being adopted.
    ISBN 0-8239-5201-0
    1. Adoption—Juvenile literature. [1. Adoption.] I. Title.
    II. Series
    HV875.H4137 1998
    362.73'4—dc21   97-47362
                                                          CIP
                                                           AC

Manufactured in the United States of America

Table of Contents

Max's Family Grows

Max's mom and dad have decided to adopt a baby. That's why Max and his mom and dad are going to the **adoption agency** (uh-DOP-shun AY-jen-see).

"Will we see where the babies live, and pick one out?" Max asked.

"Babies don't live at the agency," Mom said. "The agency is where people work to help babies and older children find families. Today we'll tell the agency that we'd like to have a child join our family."

◀ Adopting a child can be exciting for everyone in the family.

Adopting Each Other

Every baby starts by growing inside a woman's body. The day that a baby is born is the baby's birthday. The woman who gives **birth** (BERTH) to the baby is the birth mother. Sometimes a birth mother can't take care of her child. But she wants what's best for her child because she loves him or her. When that happens, she might give the child up for adoption. When a child is adopted, he or she goes to live with grown-ups who aren't the birth parents. But these grown-ups make a promise to be that child's parents every day.

Putting a newborn baby up for adoption
can be very hard for a new mother. ▶

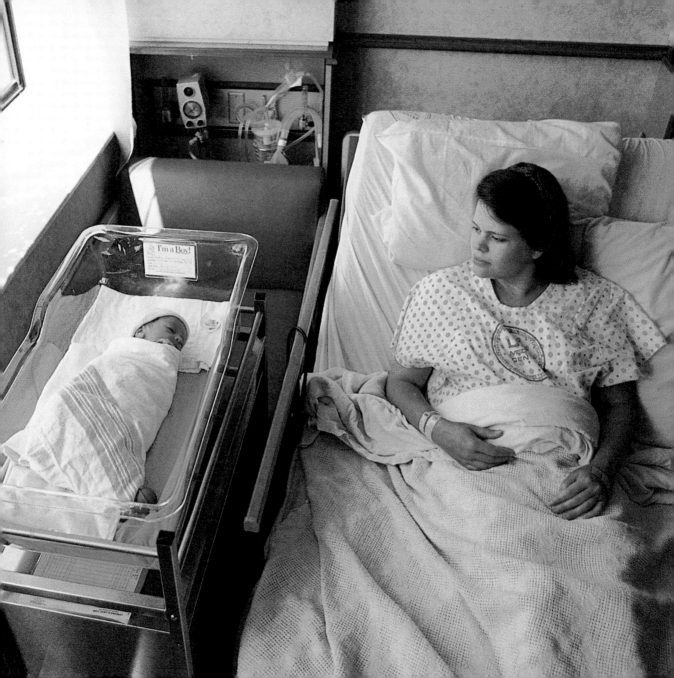

Birth Is Only the Beginning

Birth is just a short part of a baby's life. A baby's birth may only take a day or two. After the baby is born, the job of being a parent really begins. Taking care of and raising a child takes many years. It means helping whenever the child is hungry or sick. It also means teaching the child how to learn and act so he can care for himself one day. A child needs help from a grown-up for many years. And many children never stop wanting and needing their parents' love, even when they're grown-ups themselves.

◀ Kids need their parent's love throughout their entire lives.

What Babies Need

Parents give their children time, food, safety, and love. Often, those parents are birth parents. But sometimes birth parents can't care for their children. Birth parents who put their children up for adoption may not have enough money to take care of a baby. They may also be too young to raise a baby. You might think that little babies wouldn't need very much. But even babies need food and clothes and a warm, safe home. Babies may also get sick and need medicine. All of these things cost money. But most of all, babies need somebody who knows how and wants to love them.

Adoption agencies talk to people who want to adopt a child to be sure they are ready for the responsibility. ▶

Showing Love in Different Ways

Love is more than feelings. Love is shown through our actions. Parents show they love you every day by all the things they do for you. People you don't know can show love too. You may not know your birth parents, and you may think they don't love you because they gave you up for adoption. But they showed their love by making a **decision** (dih-SIH-zhun) that was best for you. They gave you to parents who could take care of you properly and love you like your birth parents do.

◀ Love is shown in many ways. Police officers show us their love by working to protect us.

People Who Love You

Sometimes you might wonder why your birth parents couldn't raise you. But knowing why they couldn't take care of you isn't as important as remembering that they found someone who could help you and love you. They made sure that you went to a place that would be safe.

The way you feel about your birth parents may change today or the next day. That's okay. You are allowed to feel however you want to.

Your adopted family is there to ▶
love you and support you.

Every Kid Is Special

If you're adopted, you might feel like you are different from kids who live with their birth parents. But you're the same as they are. You just have a different kind of parent. All kids are different from their adoptive parents. And all kids are different from their birth parents too.

Being adopted isn't what makes you different or special. You're different and special just because you're you.

◀ Just because you and your adoptive parent may look different doesn't mean your parent loves you any less.

Surprises

No parent—birth or adoptive—knows what his or her child will be like. Will she play baseball or the flute? Will he be a doctor or a teacher? Kids always surprise their parents. But parents who raise kids love them, surprises and all.

Families might have birth children, adopted children, or both. But that's not what makes people a family. Love is what makes them a family. And taking care of each other is what families do.

Whether you want to play the trumpet or walk on the moon, ▶ your family is there to support what you want to do.

Another Kind of Birthday

Everyone is special. But there are some extra-special things about being adopted. Parents who adopt a child must take a test to make sure they will be good parents. If you're adopted, your parents must be extra-special parents! Also, adopted kids often **celebrate** (SEH-luh-brayt) their birthday *and* their adoption day, or the day they were adopted. If you were born in a different country, such as Korea or Hungary, you might celebrate the day you became a **citizen** (SIH-tih-zun) of your new country too. Your family might even celebrate the holidays of your birth country!

◀ Celebrations are extra-special when families are together.

Families Are Special

Max asked his mom why she and Dad had adopted him. "Dad and I had a feeling that someone special was waiting for us," Mom said. "That someone was you."

"Did you know it was me because we match?" Max asked. Mom laughed at their family joke. Max's skin and hair were dark. Mom had fair skin and blonde hair. Mom hugged Max.

"We match on the inside," she said. "That's where matching is most important."

Glossary

adoption agency (uh-DOP-shun AY-jen-see) A place where grown-ups work to match up families who want children with children who need families.

birth (BERTH) When a baby growing in a woman's body is born.

celebrate (SEH-luh-brayt) To enjoy a special time in honor of something.

citizen (SIH-tih-zen) A person who is born in or who chooses to live in a certain country.

decision (dih-SIH-zhun) To make up your mind about something.

Index

5/05   1   10/00

19/14   (b)